HISTORY IN PICTURES

World War Two

D-DAY TO BERLIN

Robert Hamilton

Trans
Atlantic
Press

D-Day

Preparations for the invasion of Occupied France had proceeded apace in Britain throughout the winter of 1943 and the spring of 1944. The Dieppe raid in 1942 had cost many lives, but it had also shown that it was going to be virtually impossible to capture and hold a major French port. 'Operation Overlord' was therefore planned to land on the less well-defended Normandy beaches to the east of the Cherbourg peninsula. This meant that a vast invading army would have to be both deployed and supplied without the advantages of a proper harbour, so artificial 'Mulberry' harbours were built to be towed across the English Channel to the landing beaches. In preparation for the invasion, landing craft and amphibious vehicles were built, and large numbers of troops started assembling in southern Britain. In addition, a pipeline named 'PLUTO' was laid across the seabed from the Isle of Wight to Normandy to ensure this enormous army had enough oil supplies once the invasion was under way.

BELOW: Loading the landing craft required great care: although designed for the invasion and adapted for the shallow Normandy beaches, these were little more than modified barges, so their load distribution was critical. A similar design was used for different purposes: seen here are landing craft tank, the heavy version which would carry tanks as well as the half-tracks and trucks pictured. One thousand five hundred were built in the USA, many of them far inland, floated downstream to the coast and then transshipped to Britain, where some 900 were manufactured locally. These heavily laden craft crossed the English Channel under their own power, setting out from concealed positions in ports and estuaries along Britain's south coast.

OPPOSITE: A DUKW amphibious troop carrier, known to all as 'Duck', boards a tank landing ship. American-designed and built, based on a GM truck and engine, the craft could transport over water and land. Heavy-duty pumps would keep the craft afloat when holed by gunfire, and the driver could alter the air pressure in the tyres while driving, allowing the vehicle to negotiate soft sand and mud or normal road surface.

Eisenhower gives the order

The overall commander, General Eisenhower, gave the order for the long-awaited attack on the Normandy beaches to begin on 6 June 1944, D-Day. Soon after midnight a vast invasion fleet of nearly 7,000 vessels closed in on the designated beaches, and parachutists and glider-borne troops landed behind German lines in Normandy. At first light, after an initial assault from thousands of aircraft, the invasion proper began.

Five beaches were designated for the landings; the Americans landed at the westernmost beaches, codenamed 'Utah' and 'Omaha', while the British, supported by the Free French, came ashore further east at 'Gold' and 'Sword' beaches. The landing at 'Juno', in the middle of the two British beaches, was undertaken by the Canadian military, under the command of the British.

By the end of the first day some 130,000 men had landed in Occupied France and were able to establish a bridgehead in Normandy. This had come at a cost of many lives, especially at Omaha beach, where the preliminary aerial bombardment had missed the German defences along the sea wall. As the Americans came ashore, the Germans fired relentlessly from their pillboxes, gunning down hundreds of men before the beach was finally taken.

Ike encourages 101st Airborne

OPPOSITE: General Dwight D. Eisenhower talks with paratroopers of the 101st Airborne Division on 5 June prior to their embarking on their spearhead mission which would successfully secure strategic positions just beyond the Omaha beachhead in the early hours of D-Day.

The greatest armada of all time

ABOVE: Five thousand ships, manned by nearly 200,000 naval personnel, made this the largest invasion armada of all time, and on the first day more than 175,000 troops were transported, along with their armaments, transport and supplies.

Operation Overlord was planned with the utmost secrecy to ensure that the German command would continue to believe that the logical Allied invasion point would be the Pas de Calais area. Amazingly the secret was kept, even though the whole of Britain effectively became a transit and training camp for the forthcoming landings.

In sight of the shore

BELOW: The landings were arduous and dangerous for the infantry. They had to descend into landing craft down rope nets from their troop ships and in many instances wade ashore under fire – all with their full equipment. Here British troops are about to join their welcoming party of heavy armour already occupying the beachhead.

OPPOSITE: US infantry attacked on Omaha and Utah beaches next to the Cherbourg peninsula; aboard their landing craft, they are about to beach. Shells are bursting on the shore from a naval barrage but the men look calm, protected by the armoured ramp down which they will soon run to meet the enemy. These craft carried a platoon – around 30 men – possibly a jeep and, apart from the armour at the front, were mainly constructed in plywood to a design by a US timber merchant called Andrew Higgins; they were known as 'Higgins Boats'. Eisenhower said that without them the Allies would not have won the war.

DAILY MAIL JUNE 7, 1944

The last act

June 6, 1944, will stand as one of the memorable days of all time. Upon this day was launched the greatest act of war in history – the invasion of Europe. This day saw well begun the campaign which will end the war in an Allied victory.

The Germans are beaten, and they begin to know it. Rome was one portentous symbol in their darkening sky. The Allies have the advantage in men, material, morale – everything. On the Eastern Front Russia awaits her moment. No secret weapon or tactical trick can save the Third Reich now.

This is the thought that must be uppermost in our minds as we watch unfolding the gigantic combined operation of the Allied land, sea, and air forces.

'The battle,' says Mr. Churchill, 'will grow constantly in scope and intensity for many weeks to come.' It will go well at one moment and not so well at the next. The fortunes of war will not always favour us.

After nearly five years of mingled triumph and disaster the British people are not likely to be led astray by excessive hope or unreasoning despair. Rather will they respond to the words of the King, who last night asked for a revival of the crusading spirit which sustained us in the dark days.

BELOW: British troops were designated to take Gold and Sword beaches; here on Sword, near the port of Ouistreham, they form up to march towards Caen. Arromanches and Courseulles were the towns nearest Juno and Sword.

A constant stream of supplies

After the initial onslaught, the flood of men and material continued for weeks, with the Mulberry floating harbours giving moorings and protection for the supply ships. Around 600,000 military personnel would come ashore on Omaha beach as the Allied forces set about the business of reclaiming Europe.

Thanks to intensive RAF Bomber Command activity during the run-up to D-Day, the Luftwaffe was more or less neutralised, with airfields destroyed and radar knocked out. Targets were chosen with care – focus given to the Pas de Calais while systematically destroying the rail infrastructure across northern France. Under this 'smokescreen', a key gun emplacement covering Utah and Omaha beaches was bombed out by 52 RAF Lancaster planes.

Moment of surrender

OPPOSITE ABOVE: Allied troops met different levels of resistance; this US paratrooper, armed to the teeth, holds a German prisoner at bayonet point. German intelligence relating to the Allied invasion was fragmented to say the least. German Panzer units near the invasion zone delayed engagement because only Hitler could command them into action: the Führer's aides dared not wake him from sleep with news of the invasion.

OPPOSITE BELOW: French villagers look on dispassionately as German prisoners under escort are marched to prison camps at the coast.

Evacuees find safety

ABOVE: In the days following D-Day the town of Pont l'Abbé was fiercely defended by German troops, who also fought in every hedgerow and sunken lane between the town and advancing US forces. Eventually on 12 June a massive bombardment wiped out the town and the Germans moved out. French families, with a few possessions, flee their destroyed homes and try to avert their eyes from the horrors around them.

Advancing through Normandy

BELOW: The German garrison at Cherbourg numbered over 20,000 and had nowhere to go, cut off by the advancing American troops. Defeat was inevitable but their demolition squads rendered the port unusable until mid-August. The last defenders were silenced on 1 July and the captured troops were marched to the Omaha beachhead.

LEFT: In the late stages of the Allied breakout from Normandy, code-named Operation Cobra, US forces under George Patton captured the coastal town of Avranches, the gateway to Brittany. After a massive aerial bombardment and an irresistible armoured advance, Germans fled their strategic defensive positions, some of them even crossing the dangerous sands of the bay to reach Mont St Michel. Despite a fierce counterattack, the liberation of Avranches on 31 July held, allowing a rapid advance to Le Mans. Many Germans were trapped and surrendered – here a column of 2,000 prisoners is escorted by US troops.

Battle of Falaise Gap

Following the breakout from the beachhead, Allied forces began an encircling movement to trap the German armies in the area of Normandy centred on the town of Falaise. The Battle of Falaise Gap was a pivotal conflict, whereby German forces, instructed to hold their position and resist the overwhelming Allied offensive, knew they were about to be surrounded but fought desperately to keep an avenue of escape. On 21 August, the Allies finally closed the gap, trapping an estimated 50,000 Germans and leaving a clear path to Paris, which was liberated on 25 August.

OPPOSITE: The town of St-Lô in Normandy in August 1944, with not an intact building in sight. The Operation Cobra breakout had St-Lô as its first important capture – of necessity, as it was positioned on a strategic crossroads. Prior to engagement with the determined defenders, the main lines of defence were carpet-bombed then pounded by Allied artillery. American money paid for a new hospital after the war, in some recompense for the devastation. At one point it was mooted that the town should remain a ruined monument to the invasion, but it was rebuilt and its historic buildings restored.

ABOVE: The town of Falaise, the centre of two weeks of fierce fighting, is a collection of ghostly ruins, pictured here after it was finally taken by Canadian forces on 17 August.

ABOVE AND OPPOSITE: Cheering Parisians line the Champs-Elysées and applaud the thousands of Allied troops parading to celebrate the liberation of the city: a sight to feed the propaganda machine and send a message to the German High Command.

Paris liberated

The liberation of Paris was completed on 25 August after 10 days of civil and military disobedience on all sides. The Allies had no plan to liberate Paris at this stage in the war, but wanted to make all haste to Berlin to end the conflict. The large population of Paris, and intelligence reports that the German occupiers were poised to destroy the city around them, increased Allied determination to skirt round a potential Stalingrad. But a general strike from 15 August and overt action in the streets by the Free French Resistance led the French commander, General Leclerc, to disobey his battle orders from General Bradley and send an advance guard into the city with the promise of reinforcements to follow. Seeing that the die was cast, Bradley permitted Leclerc to fulfil his promise, and in the event the German commander General Dietrich von Choltitz disobeyed Hitler's orders to devastate the city, surrendering instead.

German prisoner vilified

ABOVE: Crowds jeer at this defeated German soldier marched at gunpoint through the northern town of St Mihiel, some distance east of Paris. The town would stir memories in the advancing Americans with its US Memorial Cemetery, containing the graves of over 400 American soldiers who died near by during World War I.

RIGHT: US tanks and transport line the square outside the Hôtel de Ville, providing grandstand views for the elated people of Paris who are in a party mood.

DAILY MAIL   AUGUST 26, 1944

Germans in Paris surrender

THE battle for Paris is over. General Leclerc's tank columns broke into the capital early yesterday and in less than 12 hours' fighting smashed German resistance. The end came suddenly last evening when Leclerc, according to the Patriot radio, delivered an ultimatum to the general commanding the German garrison. The two, with the Maquis chief of Paris, then went to Montparnasse Station, where the terms of the capitulation were signed.

Under these, the German general at once ordered the cease fire. His men, unarmed, were to assemble at selected points to await orders. Their arms were to be piled and handed over intact.

At about the time Leclerc dictated his terms to the German, and while fighting was still in progress, General de Gaulle entered the city. Huge crowds greeted him with the 'Marseillaise' and cries of 'Vive de Gaulle!' to which he replied: 'I wish simply and from the bottom of my heart to say to you, Vive Paris!'

Later, in a broadcast to the people of Paris, General de Gaulle declared: 'France will take her place among the great nations which will organise the peace. We will not rest until we march, as we must, into enemy territory as conquerors.' De Gaulle said that France has the 'right to insist' that she shall never again be invaded by Germany.

Brussels falls

BELOW: Retreating from the Allied advance into Brussels at the beginning of September, the fleeing Germans set the Palais de Justice ablaze. But with the Allies' capture of Antwerp soon after, it was clear to all that the battle for the lowlands was gathering momentum.

LEFT: An Allied tank crawls through the streets of newly liberated Brussels carrying many high-spirited civilian passengers. Messages of support have been chalked on to the side of the tank.

Operation
Market Garden

Montgomery's daring plan to rush mechanised forces forward to the
Rhine in the Netherlands centred on Operation Market Garden,
the largest airborne attack in history, involving over 30,000 troops,
which aimed to secure the Lower Rhine, giving a direct route into
Germany. Although brilliantly conceived, Market Garden differed
from previous Allied campaigns, with no rehearsals, no diversionary
attacks and limited tactical planning that depended on achieving a
sequence of separate objectives culminating in the taking of the bridge
over the Rhine at Arnhem. Weaknesses quickly became apparent:
commanders had ignored intelligence of German strength in the area,
radio communications failed and deadlines lagged. Men fought with
outstanding bravery and determination but at the end of the nine-day
battle on 25 September there were nearly 8,000 dead, wounded or
taken prisoner.

ABOVE: US airborne troops are pictured in their transport plane before take-off.

LEFT: Descending paratroops fill the skies, jumping from C-47 transports with their equipment.

RIGHT: Despite the steady
withdrawal of German
forces from the lowlands
of Holland and Belgium,
they continued to wreak
damage with the terrifying
V1 and V2 rockets, which
were launched many
miles from the front. Here
civilian killed in a Belgian
town are recovered by
shocked compatriots.

DAILY MAIL   NOVEMBER 9, 1944

V2 Terror in London

Hour by hour last night Germany put out claims that V2 is causing widespread damage in London. Here, said radio spokesmen, was a long-range weapon more dangerous than V1. They said it had destroyed Euston Station, smashed a railway bridge, and devastated five named areas.

Goebbels seized on V2 as a morale builder to replace the anniversary celebrations of the Munich beer cellar putsch, abandoned this year for the first time.

The weapon — neutral sources have described it as a rocket-shell 'like a flying telegraph pole with a trail of flame behind it' — was said to have been in use for some weeks. But Berlin made no mention of it until yesterday.

First came a brief reference in the High Command's communiqué and then a spate of boosting radio reports and commentaries. Among all the claims there was one significant admission – that the launching of the 'deadly weapon' caused sacrifices 'among the crews.'

The Germans claimed to be in possession of full information of the damage caused by V2. 'The British Government,' said one radio spokesman, 'has so far concealed from its people that a more effective, more telling, and therefore more dangerous long-range weapon has been in action in addition to the so-called flying bomb, which everyone knows about now.

'The German Command possess exact reports on the success and the effect of V2. If they required further proof of its accuracy, official British reports have supplied it by announcing, after nights in which London was exclusively attacked with V2, that flying bombs had again been over the capital.

'For the time being nothing further can be made known about the technical details of this missile. According to reports from England, the characteristic feature of the new weapon is that it cannot be heard or seen before its extraordinarily heavy detonation.'

Reports from Sweden and other neutral countries have credited V2 with a range of between 200 and 300 miles and a warhead of something under a ton of high explosive. Bases in Germany, Holland, Denmark, and Norway have been claimed as feasible for attacks on Britain. A rocket, it is said, would have to rise some 50 miles into the sky to achieve any considerable range, and it would travel at well over 700 miles per hour.

Smithfield Market Destroyed

BELOW: One of the worst V2 incidents of the Blitz was the devastation of Smithfield, London's historic meat and poultry market. The extensive enclosed indoor market was struck at the corner of Farringdon Street and Charterhouse Street. At 11.10 it was filled with buyers and sellers, while others were queuing outside to get in. The V2 fell out of the sky, virtually destroying the crowded building, its blast making a crater that penetrated the railway tunnel and extensive sidings running below; the casualties, commodities and rubble mingled in a horrible mêlée. The decorative ironwork that formed the intricate façade collapsed in a tangle, making rescue work even more difficult. One hundred and ten people died immediately from the blast and many more were seriously injured.

Hitler's last stand

Although the Allies had made great strides through France and Belgium, Hitler would not accept the inevitability of defeat. A fresh offensive was planned in the Ardennes where the Allied line was weakest and his new 'wonder' weapons were ready to rain down a new terror upon London.

Battle of the Bulge

The German Army launched its attack in the Ardennes in mid-December 1944. The plan was to split the Allied forces in two and create a corridor to the sea at Antwerp. The Allies managed to halt the advance on Antwerp, but not before it created a large bulge in the Allied line. The Wehrmacht found itself up against the might of the United States Army and Air Force and by January the attack had waned. The attack only served to delay the Allied invasion of Germany temporarily and came at a cost of thousands of German lives.

The conditions of fighting during the Battle of the Bulge were dreadful and although both sides showed great determination, morale was hard to maintain. In the first day of fighting, German troops overran and captured around 9,000 US troops, while German advance guard, dressed in US uniforms, set about causing confusion and chaos. On the German side, operations went awry when a parachute force was widely spread around a missed drop zone; ironically this gave the Allies the impression of a much larger attack.

BELOW: The 101st Airborne were one of the tenacious units holding Bastogne, Belgium, and fought off these unfortunate attackers whose bodies lie frozen in the snow. The Americans were in dire circumstances, down to 10 rounds of ammunition per gun per day, but fortunately the weather improved, allowing supplies to be dropped by parachute, relieving shortages of food, ammunition and medical supplies. A team of medics flew in by glider to attend to the many wounded. Eventually, elements of Patton's Third Army broke through to relieve Bastogne on 26 December.

OPPOSITE: Troops of General Patton's Third Army trudge through the winter snow in January 1945 on their way to rendezvous with Montgomery's 21st Army Group at Houffalize, Belgium, effectively closing down the German offensive – which, having suffered serious losses, was running out of steam. Hitler finally allowed his battle-weary troops to retreat on 7 January, and on 25 January the Battle of the Bulge was finally over – the most costly American military engagement to date in the war. But for Germany it was the final turning point: this gamble exhausted its military reserves and put the Luftwaffe beyond recovery.

Advancing through Germany

The early months of 1945 saw events moving fast, as the German will to fight on began to diminish. Throughout January the Russian armies advanced remorselessly upon the country from the east, liberating the Nazi concentration camp at Auschwitz on 27 January. By now it was obvious to almost everyone involved that the defeat of Germany was inevitable and imminent; and Roosevelt, Churchill and Stalin met at Yalta in the Crimea to discuss the post-war division of Germany between 4 and 11 February.

On 14 April, the Red Army took Vienna and then turned its attention towards Berlin. The Russians crossed the Oder and two armies encircled Berlin on 25 April. They joined to the west and then turned back towards the semi-ruined city, now devastated by artillery bombardment as well as heavy bombing. Meanwhile the Allies were pushing on to the Rhineland; American troops captured the bridge at Remagen intact on 7 March, at last establishing a much-needed bridgehead across the Rhine. Other Allied crossings were made and their forces now moved much further into Germany. By 12 April American troops were just sixty miles from Berlin.

YOU ARE NOW
CROSSING THE
RHINE RIVER
THROUGH COURTES
OF `E' CO. 17 ARME
ENGR. BN. AND
`C'   CO. 202
ENGR. C. BN.

Temporary crossing

OPPOSITE: US engineers constructed this pontoon bridge over the Rhine during the first day of the crossing. The 972-foot-long bridge was created in record time and was one of three that the Allied forces deployed early in Operation Plunder.

ABOVE: With the Allied forces crossing the Rhine in overwhelming numbers and using the bridges to move heavy armour into place, German opposition varied, but there was much fierce fighting and deadly machine-gun defence. Here infantry of the US 7th Army provide covering fire from the west bank of the Rhine as their fellow soldiers cross.

BELOW: Eisenhower's 'Broad Front' assault and attack over the Rhine enabled overwhelming land forces to break into Germany from the west – a crushing blow to German morale. Local commanders quickly realised their position was untenable.

Dispirited survivors

OPPOSITE ABOVE: German soldiers making a determined defence nevertheless knew that their cause was lost; furthermore they knew that if there was a choice between being captured by Americans or Russians, they would sooner give themselves up to US or British forces. Thousands of German prisoners were taken as the Allies advanced.

OPPOSITE BELOW: Around 20,000 German prisoners of war wait for marching orders in the grounds of a German military academy near the Rhine.

BELOW: Churchill visited the front line on numerous occasions to make a personal appraisal of the situation and to encourage his forces. On 25 March he arrived at Montgomery's HQ and, with him and a number of US officers, crossed the Rhine by boat to an area still controlled by German forces; targeted by artillery, they swiftly withdrew.

DAILY MAIL   MARCH 9, 1945

The Rhine crossed

We've done it. Early this morning strong infantry forces of General Hodge's American First Army are streaming across the Rhine into our newly won bridgehead on the east bank of the river. The final drive to meet the Russian armies in the heart of Germany – the last heave to end the war – has begun.

You can throw your hats in the air to-day. The success of our lightning stroke undoubtedly shortens the war by months. We are massing substantial forces in our rapidly expanding bridgehead 290 miles from Berlin.

This historic moment in the war came at 4.30 p.m. on Wednesday, when a spearhead task force of the First Army crossed the river in a sudden thrust which took the Germans completely by surprise. The crossing was made between Bonn and Coblenz. Opposition was light. Once on the other side the Americans spread out to get elbow-room. Then our main forces poured over. Before their tremendous onslaught the German defences cracked – then collapsed like a pack of cards.

More and more men swarmed across the river, and swiftly, efficiently, the bridgehead was built up.

Hitler tried to rally his troops on 30 March with a message encouraging 'fanatic determination' to defend Berlin and achieve victory. Whether anybody believed his words, many Germans fought on – especially on the Eastern Front, where the Russian advance was

Allies pour into Germany

BELOW: British infantry advance into Germany on foot after crossing the Rhine.

OPPOSITE ABOVE: Densely packed German prisoners of war are guarded vigilantly under the sights of this US soldier's machine gun.

OPPOSITE BELOW: The fortifications of Jülich led to its being bombed to oblivion by the advancing Allies, who assumed that the town, located strategically on the River Rur, a tributary to the Meuse, would be a major obstacle to their advance. Churchill visited the town after it had been captured, and Eisenhower was also photographed among the ruins.

Bombing Germany's industrial heartland

RIGHT: A mixture of high explosive and incendiary bombs descends on Gladbeck in the industrial Ruhr region of Germany. Gladbeck's railway marshalling yards were vital to the distribution of coal from the town's mines. 1,250 B-17s and B-24s of the Eighth USAAF carried out the raid on 23 March, escorted by 350 P-51 Mustang fighter aircraft.

BELOW: Citizens of Saarbrucken congregate with their few possessions in the centre of the destroyed city. Most of its population of 135,000 fled in the face of the Allied aerial onslaught and ground attack in March 1945.

RIGHT: This 14-year-old German boy soldier was captured in the March assault on the Siegfried Line. With Wehrmacht military reserves exhausted, the Volkssturm militia provided combat troops from their ranks of juveniles and retirees.

BELOW: British and Canadian troops spread south-eastwards from the lowlands of Holland and Belgium, reaching Udem, east of the Rhine, on 27 February then moving on to capture Kervenheim. Here British infantry brew up outside Udem while a rifleman keeps lookout.

PoWs released

ABOVE: Altengrabow Camp, Stalag XIA, housed 20,000 Allied prisoners, including 2,000 British and Americans. It was first used in World War I and the conditions were poor and overcrowded; just before liberation there was an outbreak of typhus. By this point in the war, Germany was very short of food and the prisoners were starving.

LEFT: British PoWs in April 1945, after being liberated from Stalag 11B near Fallingbostel; all the prisoners were suffering from malnutrition and had to be weaned carefully back to a normal diet. Red Cross parcels were sent to all PoW camps and should have been distributed in accord with the Geneva Convention. In reality, most were diverted by the German authorities.

OPPOSITE BELOW: British soldiers liberated Belsen concentration camp on 15 April. Thousands of people were found still alive but threatened by typhus, typhoid and dysentery, which were running rampant in the camp.

The Nazi regime subscribed to the belief that the German people sat atop a global racial hierarchy and that other races – particularly Jews but also gypsies and Slavs – were inferior and a threat to German racial purity. After they came to power in 1933, the Nazis had begun an incremental process of government-sponsored persecution of the country's Jewish population. They passed laws to deny Jews of their citizenship, to forbid them from marrying Aryans and to force them out of their jobs and businesses. The night of 9 November 1938, 'Kristallnacht', witnessed the first coordinated nationwide attack against Jews; many of Germany's synagogues were damaged and people were rounded up and sent to concentration camps. The following year, the war intervened and Germany's treatment of the Jews took an even deadlier turn.

Allied troops advancing through Germany began their discovery of the gruesome Nazi death camps; the PoW camps were bad enough, but the dawning realisation of the scale of the Nazi extermination programme horrified the world. Josef Kramer, nicknamed the Beast of Belsen, was captured at Bergen-Belsen (right). He was tried for war crimes, convicted and hanged in December 1945.

Horror of death camps

LEFT: The liberation of the Nazi prison camps presented a huge challenge to the Allies; the prisoners were in terrible physical condition and continued to die in large numbers after being liberated. Of those that survived, most were vast distances from their homes, which very probably had been destroyed, along with relatives, neighbours or other possible support for these shattered people. Repatriating Allied PoWs was relatively straightforward, but the civilians generally continued to live in camps, moving from concentration camps into displaced-persons centres, while the Red Cross and other organisations supported their search for lost relatives and a way to return home.

OPPOSITE BELOW: The German military authorities understood how the Allies would view the death camps, and some efforts were made to conceal them. In the last months of the war, concentration camps in the East of Germany and Poland were evacuated, their occupants forced to march deep into Germany under terrible conditions that killed many thousands. Here a mass grave is uncovered – the last resting place of prisoners on their way to Bergen-Belsen who died in transit. They were buried by surviving inmates, who were then shot and added to the burial.

BELOW: Photographs like this helped people understand the scale and horror of the death camps: the personal possessions of the murdered inmates, such as these shoes, were stockpiled in storage in their tens of thousands.

From October 1939, as the Nazis consolidated their control of Poland, the country's large Jewish population had been forced to live in walled-off ghettoes where thousands of people died of starvation and disease. After the invasion of the Soviet Union in June 1941, the Nazis began directly killing Jews using mobile killing units called 'Einsatzgruppen', which murdered more than one million men, women and children behind the German lines. In late 1941 Nazis began constructing death camps and by early 1942 they had decided upon a 'Final Solution': the extermination of all the Jews of Europe. Millions of people were sent to death camps such as Auschwitz, Treblinka, Sobibor and Belzec, where they were murdered in specially designed gas chambers. The 'lucky ones' were sent to work camps, where they faced gruelling labour and death from disease, hunger and maltreatment. By 1945, as Allied soldiers closed in on the camps, thousands of inmates were moved by train or on forced 'death marches' to prevent them from being liberated and to prolong their suffering. By the time the war was over, more than six million Jews had lost their lives, an estimated two-thirds of Europe's pre-war Jewish population.

In addition, the Nazis dehumanised, detained and murdered hundreds of thousands of other people deemed to be racially undesirable or politically unsound. These groups included gypsies, homosexuals and Communists, as well as people with physical or mental illnesses who were also subjected to forcible sterilisations as part of a campaign of so-called 'racial hygiene'.

Allies link up

BELOW: On 25 April, US and Soviet troops linked up at the town of Torgau on the River Elbe. This photograph, staged for the press, had great symbolism for the Allied world: the handshake of infantry on the demolished bridge showed that a shattered Europe could be restored.

OPPOSITE BELOW: In northern Germany, close to the River Elbe, mechanised troops of the 15th Scottish Division enveloped then cleared the town of Uelzen on 19 April. Uelzen hosted a concentration camp and was strategically placed on the Mittelland Canal.

Reichstag

OPPOSITE ABOVE: The link-up of the Allied armies sealed the fate of an overwhelmed Germany, everywhere in ruins. Like the Reichstag parliament building in Berlin pictured here, Hitler's glorious Third Reich was now an empty shell.

Victory in Europe

By mid-April 1945, Russian troops were fighting their way through Berlin street by street, heading towards the Reichstag. Hitler may have ordered 'fanatic determination' from all Germans in the defence of Berlin, but he retreated to his underground bunker on 16 April and began to lose his grip on reality. On 30 April, after nominating Admiral Karl Dönitz as his successor and blaming the Jews for the war, Hitler and his new wife Eva Braun committed suicide. On the same day, above ground, the battle for Berlin was won and the Soviet flag fluttered atop the ruins of the Reichstag building. The following day Hitler's propaganda minister Joseph Goebbels and his wife supervised the deaths of their six children before killing themselves. The remains of the German armies now began to surrender and, on 7 May, General Eisenhower formally accepted the unconditional surrender of Germany. VE Day was celebrated across the world the

ABOVE: Spirits ran high in London with the announcement by Winston Churchill on 8 June that the war in Europe was at an end. Westminster and the West End of London filled with jubilant people; forming a human pyramid on a truck held no fear for those who had survived the Blitz!

Celebrating in Times Square, Red Square and Trafalgar Square

BELOW: The announcement of VE Day brought thousands of Americans into New York City's Times Square to celebrate the unconditional surrender of Germany.

LEFT: Marshal Joseph Stalin ordered a victory parade in Red Square on 24 June – a massive military display that honoured Soviet Marshals Zhukov and Rokossovsky and culminated in captured Nazi banners being cast down in front of the Mausoleum.

VICTORY OVER GERMANY 1945

GIVE THANKS BY SAVING

DAILY MAIL   MAY 9, 1945

VE Day – it's all over

London, dead from six until nine, suddenly broke into victory life last night. Suddenly, spontaneously, deliriously. The people of London, denied VE-Day officially, held their own jubilation. 'VE-Day may be tomorrow,' they said, 'but the war is over to-night.' Bonfires blazed from Piccadilly to Wapping.

The sky once lit by the glare of the blitz shone red with the Victory glow. The last trains departed from the West End unregarded. The pent-up spirits of the throng, the polyglot throng that is London in war-time, burst out, and by 11 o'clock the capital was ablaze with enthusiasm.

Processions formed up out of nowhere, disintegrating for no reason, to re-form somewhere else. Waving flags, marching in step, with linked arms or half-embraced, the people strode down the great thoroughfares – Piccadilly, Regent-street, the Mall, to the portals of Buckingham Palace.

They marched and counter-marched so as not to get too far from the centre. And from them, in harmony and discord, rose song. The songs of the last war, the songs of a century ago. The songs of the beginning of this war – 'Roll out the Barrel' and 'Tipperary'; 'Ilkla Moor' and 'Loch Lomond'; 'Bless 'em All' and 'Pack Up Your Troubles.'

Welcome Home

OPPOSITE: The crowds in Trafalgar Square stand silently listening to the words of King George VI that were being relayed from Buckingham Palace to a local Tannoy system. Ecstatic crowds cheered the Royal Family, who waved from the Palace balcony.

ABOVE: This British sergeant, recently released from a German PoW camp, is greeted by his family and receives a hero's welcome in his Devon village. Spick and span in a new uniform and smiling broadly, no one could guess the ordeal men like him had been through during their incarceration.

This is a Transatlantic Press Book
First published in 2012

Transatlantic Press
38 Copthorne Road, Croxley Green, Hertfordshire, UK

© Atlantic Publishing

Photographs © Associated Newspapers Archive

A catalogue record for this book is available from the British Library.

ISBN 978-1-908849-06-9

Printed in China